Edmund Lyon

The Lyon Phonetic Manual

Edmund Lyon

The Lyon Phonetic Manual

ISBN/EAN: 9783337429645

Printed in Europe, USA, Canada, Australia, Japan

Cover: Foto ©Thomas Meinert / pixelio.de

More available books at **www.hansebooks.com**

AMERICAN ASSOCIATION TO PROMOTE THE
TEACHING OF SPEECH TO THE DEAF.

———•———

CIRCULAR OF INFORMATION No. 2, 1891.

———•———

THE LYON PHONETIC MANUAL,

— BY —

EDMUND LYON.

———•———

ROCHESTER, N. Y.:
PRINTED AT THE DEAF-MUTE INSTITUTION.
1891.

TO

MY SILENT BROTHERS AND SISTERS

IN THE HOPE THAT

IT MAY HELP TO SOFTEN THE LINE WHICH SEPARATES THEM

FROM THE HEARING WORLD

I DEDICATE THIS PHONETIC MANUAL.

CONTENTS.

PREFACE.

THE American Association to Promote the Teaching of Speech to the Deaf, has very graciously and very courteously placed at my disposal one of their CIRCULARS OF INFORMATION with the expressed desire that I should, through its pages, present to all interested in educational work, and especially to those interested in the methods of instruction among the deaf, the results of my labors on a Phonetic Manual which was perfected, during the past school year, through constant practical use and experiment at the Western New York Institution for Deaf-Mutes at Rochester.

In this exposition substantially the same treatment will be adopted which was observed in outlining the unfinished Manual before the Twelfth Convention of American Instructors of the Deaf, held in New York City, in August, 1890. I will give first a short history of the manner in which it was developed, then a detailed description of the Manual with the principles underlying it, and finally a few words in regard to its aims and practical workings.

I am indebted to Prof. Alexander Melville Bell for generously permitting me to use the physiological charts shown on page 13, which are reproduced from "Sounds and their Relations." It is with Prof. Bell's knowledge and sanction that the Visible Speech symbols are shown in connection with the Manual positions.

6

I desire to express my grateful appreciation to all who have shown a friendly interest in the Manual, and especially to Prof. Z. F. Westervelt and Miss Harriette E. Hamilton for their hearty support and kindly words of encouragement, which have done so much to lighten the labor as well as enhance the pleasure of the task.

6 South Fitzhugh Street,
Rochester, N. Y.
June, 1891.

INTRODUCTION.

IT is sometimes interesting to follow the development even of those schemes which we may not be fully prepared to endorse. So, perhaps, the most agreeable way in which there can be afforded a general apprehension of this Manual and the reasons for its existence, is to give the history of its development as it has advanced, step by step, from arbitrary and unsuggestive letters up to speaking symbols. The word "speaking" is here used because in the Manual under consideration a signification attaches to the different parts of the hand, so that each position has a story to tell for those who understand its language. The several positions of the hand, now, not only represent various speech sounds, but have embodied within them a clear and concise statement of the way in which the represented sound is physiologically or mechanically produced.

More than two years ago I began the preparation of a manual which should have for its chief recommendation, speed ; but as the work advanced its scope widened until finally the results, which are represented in the series of Charts now shown, were attained. At the outset my qualifications for the task were very meagre. They consisted principally in a practical knowledge of Phono-Stenography, a very imperfect idea of the educational methods employed among the deaf, and a wholly incorrect notion regarding the ease and rapidity with which they could express their thoughts. Had I been aware, at that time, that the deaf already had great facility of intercommunication, and that a speed of from 125 to 250 words per minute could be attained by means of the common manual alphabet, I should have certainly hesitated a long time before attempting the inauguration of any improvement. It seemed to me, however, from my then limited observation, that the facility of intercommunication among the deaf was not what it should be, and might be greatly improved.

In many respects the eye is superior to the ear, and is capable of recognizing nicer distinctions. This is illustrated in a comparison of the powers of the eye and the ear, in the detection of shades of color on the part of the one, and in the detection of pitch on the part of the other. It seemed, therefore, that the deaf were not lacking in ability to perceive and apprehend visibly represented speech sounds, but were in need of a more perfect mode of representing such sounds. If only a method could be discovered whereby their dexterity in representing sounds would be made commensurate with their power of perceiving them, the greatest possible facility for the interchange of thought would be attained.

My experience in the use of Phonography had shown me that it was possible to transmute speech sounds into legible characters, as rapidly as they could be uttered ; and afterward, with the same rapidity, to re-transmute the written characters into the original sounds. This suggested the advisability of calling the phonetic principle into requisition : and I at once began to devise my first manual, which had for its foundation that loose but practical analysis of speech sounds employed in ordinary short-hand writing. The positions of the hand used in the common manual were retained as far as available, and modified or replaced only when incompatible with an easy and rapid transition from one position to another. To this end especial study and attention were given to the sequence of sounds as they occur in spoken words. This also was borne in mind in the selecting of new positions to represent the sounds not previously symbolized. The primary object of the manual was attained to such an extent that, with a few weeks' practice, I was able to spell at the rate of 115 words per minute ; whereas a very much longer use of the old manual had enabled me to spell only at the rate of 80 words per minute.

In the spring of 1890 this manual came accidentally to the notice of Prof. Z. F. Westervelt, Principal of the Rochester Institution. He saw in it sufficient merit to warrant him in making an experimental use of it in his school. He did not attach so much importance to the fact that the manual was speedy, as to the fact that it was a phonetic manual ; that it provided a convenient and ever present mode of representing words as spoken, and of giving to each sound a positive and invariable symbol,—thus affording a certain stimulus to the memory of the deaf and aiding them in their efforts at articulation.

It soon became apparent, however, to both the faculty and myself tlfat the new manual, although possessing some excellencies, failed to have many other qualities of importance. It was phonetic, but extremely circumscribed. Its positions represented invariably the same sounds, but those positions gave no hint regarding the formation of the sounds. I therefore abandoned this manual entirely and started anew, having become fully persuaded that no amount of patching would make it satisfactory to the profession.

This time I built on a more worthy foundation. I did myself the honor of following Prof. Alexander Melville Bell's exquisite analysis as set forth in Visible Speech, which is so simple and yet so exhaustive.

To devise a single-hand manual which should provide the hundred or more positions required to represent Prof. Bell's analysis of Consonants, Vowels, and Glides, appeared an utter impossibility. Much experimenting and study, however, caused the difficulties gradually to disappear ; so that in the end it was found possible to place the hand in upward of one hundred and twenty positions, all of which could be readily assumed and easily distinguished from one another, and all of which would be in perfect harmony with certain general underlying principles. So perfectly adapted was the hand found to represent the functions of the vocal organs that it seemed to sustain toward them some mystic relation.

Not only were positions found, which would clearly set forth all of the characteristics involved in Prof. Bell's scheme of Consonants, Vowels, Glides, and Combinations ; but twenty-four additional positions are provided, which are denominated Glides-Indicated. These may be assumed after the proper Vowel position by an easy transition, so that the Vowel position merges into them by a gliding movement, thereby portraying the actual operation of the vocal organs in passing from a Vowel to its Glide, or vanish.

All of these positions appear on the Charts which accompany this paper. In the preparation of these Charts great pains has been taken to make them in all respects acceptable. So difficult was it to obtain uniformity*in the representation of the positions, and in excellency of workmanship, that nearly six hundred negatives had to be made before satisfactory photographs, for the engraver to work from, could be obtained. All of the positions are supposed to be seen from a common point of view ; the point of view being in front of, and diagonally opposite, the hand used by the operator. The student, when practicing alone, should place himself at a slight angle to his mirror, so that the hand which he employs will be farthest from it : this will enable him to duplicate perfectly the positions as represented on the Charts.

PHONETIC MANUAL.

EXPLANATORY DIAGRAM.

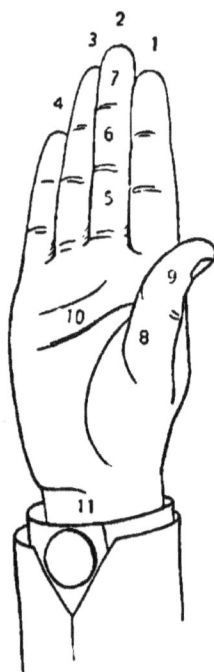

1 The first or index finger. *2.* The second or middle finger. *3.* The third finger. *4.* The fourth finger. *5.* The finger's first or lower phalanx. *6.* The finger's second phalanx. *7.* The finger's upper or terminal phalanx. *8.* The thumb's second or breath phalanx. *9.* The thumb's terminal or voice phalanx. *10.* The palm. *11.* The wrist.

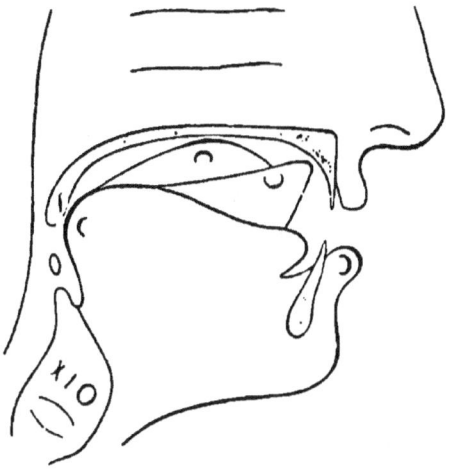

CONSONANTS.

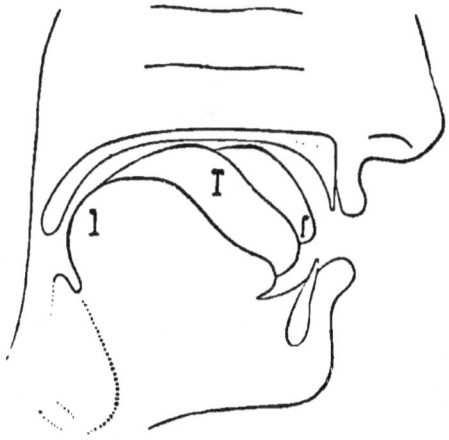

VOWELS.

GENERAL PRINCIPLES GOVERNING THE DEVELOPMENT OF THE MANUAL.

The positions of the hand are, as intimated, descriptive of the vocal organs and their functions ; so, in order to understand the Manual thoroughly, it will be necessary to hold clearly in mind certain fundamental facts regarding those organs and their action in the production of articulate sounds. The speech sounds, which the Manual representations embrace, are grouped under the three-fold classification of Consonants, Vowels, and Glides. These three classes of sounds are distinguished from one another by reason of certain organic differences in the manner of their formation. Consonants have a closed or narrowly expanded adjustment of the vocal organs, so that in their production some part of the throat or mouth obstructs, squeezes, or divides the breath. Vowels have a wide, firm, and free channel, whereby the breath is modified without friction or sibilation. Glides are only transitional sounds. They are intermediate to Consonants and Vowels, combining the characteristics of certain central-aperture Consonants with the wide or expanded quality of Vowels, but differing from Vowels in not having a fixed configuration. In representing each of these classes of sounds, a peculiar and exclusive mode of accenting or making prominent the important or telling parts of the hand is resorted to, so that, when the different ways of accentuation are understood, the class to which a given position belongs may be readily determined. The modes of accentuation adopted, impart to the various Manual positions something more than mere arbitrary class distinction. A hint at the physiological differences between Consonants, Vowels, and Glides also is given, when the positions that represent them are viewed from the index-finger side of the hand, and the fingers are considered which are accented or made prominent, according to the rules presently to be stated. It will then be apparent, that in representing Consonants the hand suggests

a narrow adjustment of the organs, by having the prominent or accented fingers straightened and the second phalanx of the thumb close to the plane of the palm [see cut
8, page 20, and cut 10, page 21]; and that in representing
Vowels the hand suggests a wide and firm channel, by
having the accented finger bent and its terminal phalanx
brought firmly in contact with the terminal phalanx of the
thumb [see cuts 12 and 16, pages 24, 26]. It also will be
found that in representing Glides the peculiarities of Consonants and Vowels are blended : the accented fingers, by
being straightened, contribute a Consonant characteristic ;
while the second phalanx of the thumb, by being held at an
angle to the plane of the palm, imparts to the Glide positions the wide, without giving them the firm, quality of
Vowel positions [see cut 26, page 31]. These organic differences which exist between Consonants, Vowels, and
Glides, and the manner of their illustration in the Manual,
will be again referred to when we come to discuss separately
the several classes of speech sounds.

In the representation
of Consonants, Vowels,
and Glides the positions
are divided, so far as it is
found to be practicable,
into posterior and ante-
rior, according to the
location of the parts of
the vocal organs which
principally mould these
sounds. In accordance
with this classification,
one position of the palm
is invariably employed
to represent posterior

No. 1.
Non-Vocal Back Shut
Consonant,
[k in like].

No. 2.
Non-Vocal Lip
Shut Consonant,
[p in rip].

positions [see cut 1], and another position of the palm
is invariably employed to represent anterior positions [see
cut 2]; or, to speak specifically, whenever the palm is held

16

laterally at an angle to the arm some posterior position is indicated, and whenever the palm is held upright and in line with the arm some anterior position is indicated. The reason for selecting these two positions of the palm for this purpose, will be discovered when they are considered in connection with the location of the several parts of the vocal organs, as shown on a physiological chart similar to those on page 13. When the right fore-arm, held so as to expose the palm, is placed perpendicularly against such a chart, directly below the anterior portion of the vocal organs thereon shown ; the palm will be directed toward the posterior positions when it is held laterally at an angle to the arm, and toward the anterior positions when it is held upright and in line with the arm.

No. 3.
Vocalized Lip Nasal Consonant,
[*m* in home].

No. 4.
Vocalized Lip Shut Consonant,
[*b* in rib].

The second and terminal phalanges of the thumb also have a constant value and meaning throughout the Manual. The manner in which the breath is used is disclosed by the position of the second phalanx. When it is carried out beyond the index-finger side of the hand and is out of contact [see cut 3], it represents the breath as passing into the nose, or Nasality. When the breath phalanx occupies any other position it represents the breath as passing into the mouth [see cut 4]. The terminal phalanx of the thumb always relates to voice. Whenever the breath is accompanied with voice this upper or terminal phalanx of the thumb is brought in line with the second or breath phalanx, and is then termed accented ; and whenever the breath is unaccompanied with voice the terminal phalanx is bent at right angles to the second phalanx, and is then termed unaccented [see cuts 4 and 2, pages 16, 15].

Hence, the Non-Vocal Consonants and the Breath-Glide have the voice phalanx of the thumb unaccented ; while the Vocalized Consonants, the Vowels, and the Glides, with the single exception of the Breath-Glide, always have the voice phalanx of the thumb accented.

Another principle of general application is, that straightened fingers which are unaccented simply signify " Wide." This feature is often called into use when it is necessary to distinguish between two sounds which are organically alike in all respects, except that the production of one is attended with a comparatively wider expansion of some portion of the vocal organs.

Having discussed speech sounds generally, and having called attention to the most important features and principles, which are of universal application throughout the Manual, we are now prepared to examine the representation of the several classes individually, and to see how the principles of Visible Speech are therein further exemplified.

CONSONANTS.

We will consider first the Consonant positions and observe how they indicate the various Consonant characteristics. Consonant positions are distinguished by having the breath phalanx of the thumb close to the plane of the palm and the accented fingers, when there are any, straightened. The terminal or voice phalanx of the thumb when accented, that is, held in line with its second phalanx, is never permitted to come in contact with the second or with the terminal phalanx of any accented finger ; so that these fingers when viewed laterally have a thin aspect, which corresponds

to the narrow adjustment of the vocal organs in the production of the represented sounds [see cuts 8 and 10,
pages 20, 21]. Two varieties of Consonants, the Shut and
the Nasal, as we shall see presently, are represented without
the aid of significant or accented fingers [see cuts 3 and 4,
page 16]; but, as accented fingers are not totally wanting
in any of the positions under Vowels, Glides, or Glides-Indicated, this fact of itself serves to identify all such Manual
positions as Consonant positions.

<table>
</table>

No. 5.   No. 6.
[Aspirate Position.]   [Guttural Contraction.]
Non-Vocal Throat Primary Consonants.

In reading a position which represents a Consonant formation, we begin at the index-finger side of the hand and
treat as accented the nearest straightened finger, and also
all other straightened fingers which are directly or indirectly in contact therewith ; and as unaccented, all fingers
which are not straightened, and also all straightened fingers
which are out of contact with an accented finger. As
heretofore stated, straightened unaccented fingers simply
signify "Wide." The only instance where a "Wide" significance is imparted to a Consonant position by means of
straightened unaccented fingers, is found in the Non-Vocal
Throat Primary. There are two Non-Vocal Throat Primary

Consonant positions ; of these the one which represents the
aspirate has the " Wide " feature [see cut 5, page 18], while
the one which represents guttural contraction does not have
that feature [see cut 6, page 18].

Consonants are broadly classified as Non-Vocal and Vocalized. In all Non-Vocal positions the voice phalanx of
the thumb is unaccented [see cut 2, page 15], and in all Vocalized positions the voice phalanx is accented [see cut 4,
page 16]. This is in accordance with the general rule, that
whenever the breath is accompanied with voice the terminal phalanx of the thumb, which always refers to voice,
is accented, that is, brought in line with the second phalanx ; and whenever the breath is unaccompanied with
voice the terminal phalanx is bent at right angles to the
second phalanx, or unaccented. By referring to the Charts
it will be seen that the position of the voice phalanx of the
thumb constitutes the only distinguishing feature between
analogous Non-Vocal and Vocalized Consonants. In other
words, the Vocalized are duplicates of analogous Non-Vocal
Consonants in every respect except as to the position of
the voice phalanx of the thumb, which with the former is
accented, and with the latter is unaccented.

In the formation of Consonant sounds the Throat, which
will be a subject for future consideration, the Back of the
tongue, the Top of the tongue, the Point of the tongue,
and the Lip, are chiefly concerned. The Back and Top of
the tongue are regarded as posterior, and the Point of the
tongue and the Lip as anterior. Consequently, in all of the
Back and Top positions the palm is held laterally at an angle
to the fore-arm to denote posterior positions, while in all of
the Point and Lip positions the palm is held upright and in
line with the arm to denote anterior positions. This will be
more fully understood by reference to the Charts. It should
be observed, that in changing the hand from a posterior to
an anterior position, or *vice versa*, the palm always remains
in the same plane : and that the arm is held substantially
motionless, being permitted neither to twist nor to sway.

No. 7.   No. 8.
[VIEWED BY OBSERVER.]   [VIEWED BY OPERATOR.]
Vocalized Lip Mixed-Divided Consonant.

In the Manual the Back positions are distinguished from
the Top positions, and the Lip positions are distinguished
from the Point positions, by the direction which the lower
phalanges of the fingers take relatively to the palm. The
Back and the Lip positions have the lower phalanges of the
fingers in the same plane as the palm [see cuts 7 and
8], while the Top and the Point positions have the
lower phalanges of the fingers at right angles to the palm
[see cuts 9 and 10. page 21]. It will be seen therefore that the
Back positions are exactly like the Lip positions, except that
with the Back positions the palm is held laterally at an angle
to the arm to indicate that they are posterior, while with
the Lip positions the palm is held upright and in line with
the arm to indicate that they are anterior. The same relation exists between the Top and the Point positions. This
resemblance of the Back positions to the Lip positions, and
of the Top positions to the Point positions, is in harmony
with the fact, that when, in the formation of Consonant sounds. the Back of the tongue is not employed
alone, it is usually mixed or used in conjunction with the

Lip, and *vice versa;* and when the Top of the tongue is mixed it is usually mixed with the Point of the tongue, and *vice versa.*

No. 9.
[VIEWED BY OBSERVER.]

No. 10.
[VIEWED BY OPERATOR.]

Vocalized Point Mixed-Divided Consonant,
[*th* in wi*th*].

The location of the Throat differs principally from that of the Back of the tongue by being lower. The Manual Throat positions are therefore similar to the Back positions, but have the index finger separated from the other fingers, which in effect deflects them, and apparently directs their first phalanges to a point below that indicated by the Back positions [see cuts 5 and 6, page 18]. Hence, the only distinguishing characteristic in the Manual between the Back and the Throat positions is, that with the former the fingers are all held in contact with one another, while with the latter the index and middle fingers are never permitted to come in contact with each other.

Having fully described the five general positions of the hand which indicate the Throat, the Back, Top, and Point of the tongue, and the Lip, it now remains for us to examine the differentiations of those general positions with their significations.

In all of these general positions the second and terminal phalanges of the fingers and the thumb are still available with which to make specific modifications. Beginners should be careful, in changing the positions of the second and terminal phalanges of the fingers, not to throw the first or lower phalanges out of position. These latter phalanges should always be parallel, and should be either in the plane of the palm, or at right angles thereto ; a failure in any of these particulars will result in the formation of anomalous and meaningless positions.

A glance along the perpendicular columns of the Consonant Charts will disclose the fact that the representations are to a certain extent mono-symbolic. Each subdivision will be found to have a common distinguishing modification or class characteristic :—Primary Consonants have one finger accented ; Mixed Consonants have three ; Divided Consonants have two ; Mixed-Divided Consonants have four ; etc. As an invariable signification attaches to all these modifications throughout the Consonant positions, they will be generally discussed.

The first and second fingers, when accented, are descriptive of the character of the opening at the point indicated by the general position of the hand. When one, and only one, of these fingers is accented the aperture is represented as single and central, or Primary. When both of these fingers are accented the aperture is represented as consisting of two parts, or Divided. When neither of these fingers is accented the aperture is inferentially indicated as being, at the inception of the sound, wholly wanting, or Shut.

The Shut positions may be transformed into Nasal positions simply by moving the second phalanx of the thumb away from the side of the hand ; because the second phalanx of the thumb always relates to the manner in which the breath is used, and only when that phalanx is carried out beyond the side of the hand and is out of contact does it represent the breath as passing into the nose, or Nasality. It will be remembered that when this phalanx of the thumb occupies any other position it represents the breath as passing into the mouth. In assuming oral Consonant positions the second phalanx of the thumb should be held parallel to the index-finger side of the palm [see cut 19, page 28], and never should be permitted to lie diagonally across the palm, as shown in cuts 21 and 23, on pages 29 and 30. In representing oral Non-Vocal Consonants the voice phalanx of the thumb should always be in a position where it will be grasped only by the index finger, when the hand is closed [see cuts 5 and 6, page 18, and cut 29, page 47].

The third and fourth fingers indicate that the Consonant is, or is not, Mixed. When both of these fingers are accented we are given to understand, that two parts of the mouth are used in conjunction to produce the represented sound, and that the part indicated by the general position of the hand is primary and the other secondary or auxiliary. Thus when one, and only one, of the fingers which are descriptive of the aperture, is accented at the same time that the third and fourth fingers are accented, a Mixed Consonant is represented ; and when all the fingers are accented, a Mixed-Divided Consonant is represented.

The general Consonant positions with their modifications. as above described, provide a way for representing fifty-two positions of the vocal organs.

VOWELS.

Vowel positions are thirty-six in number, and are distinguished generally from Consonants, Glides, and Glides-Indicated by the way of accenting the finger which is to receive primary attention. This accentuation consists in bringing the accented voice phalanx of the thumb in contact with the terminal phalanx of the finger to be accented, in such a way as to cause all the phalanges of the finger and thumb to lie as nearly as possible in the same plane [see cut 22, page 29]. Perhaps it should be stated. that this mode of accentuation may not co-exist with the one explained in connection with Consonants, Glides. and Glides-Indicated. and that the one just described always takes precedence. In other words. the strongest accent which can be given. is effected when attention is directed to a finger by bringing

the voice phalanx of the thumb, when accented, properly in contact therewith ; and whenever this is done all
straightened fingers, if there be any, are immediately
robbed of their accent and specific attributes, so that they
become unaccented straightened fingers possessing the
single general attribute " Wide." The voice phalanx of the
thumb when unaccented, is never employed to accent a finger. By reason of the manner of accenting employed, the
Vowel positions are firmer, and, as viewed by the operator, wider than the Consonant positions ; so that, as already
explained, they incidentally hint at the physiological difference between Vowels and Consonants [compare cut 8,
page 20, with cut 12].

No. 11.
[VIEWED BY OBSERVER.]

No. 12.
[VIEWED BY OPERATOR.]

Low Front Primary Vowel,
[e in net].

In representing Primary Vowels the accented voice phalanx of the thumb and the terminal phalanx of the accented
finger overlap. Straightened unaccented fingers are never
employed. [See cuts 11 and 12.]

Wide Vowels differ from analogous Primary Vowels in
having their production attended with a wider expansion
of the vocal organs. From the general principle that the
" Wide " significance is contributed by straightened unaccented fingers, it logically follows, that in the representation

of all Primary Vowels the unaccented fingers are closed. and that in the representation of all the Wide Vowels at least one of the unaccented fingers is straightened [see cut 11, page 24, and cut 13]. The selection of the finger, or fingers, for this purpose, has been influenced chiefly by ease of manipulation, and of transition to and from other positions.

No. 13.
Low Front Wide Vowel,
[ɹ in ɑt].

No. 14.
Low Back Primary Round Vowel,
[ɹ in fɑll].

Each of the Primary and Wide Vowels may be changed into an analogous Round Vowel by "rounding" the voice channel. Round Vowels are therefore visibly distinguished from normal aperture Primary and Wide Vowels by a contraction of the labial aperture. This lip modification is represented in the Manual by bringing the tips of the terminal phalanges of the thumb and accented finger together so as to form an outline which is approximately round [see cut 14, and cut 32, page 49].

Vowels are appropriately designated as Back, Front, and Mixed accordingly as the parts of the mouth which are principally concerned in their formation are posterior, anterior, or intermediate. Hence, in representing Back Vowels the palm is always held laterally at an angle to the arm

to indicate a posterior position [see cut 15]; in representing Front Vowels the palm is held upright and in
line with the arm to indicate an anterior position [see cuts 11
and 12, page 24]; while in representing Mixed Vowels the

No. 15.
[VIEWED BY OBSERVER.]

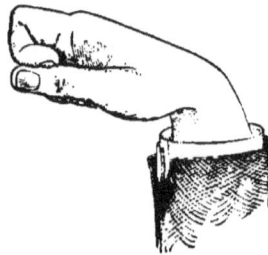

No. 10.
[VIEWED BY OPERATOR.]

Low Back Primary Vowel.

wrist is bent so as to throw the palm directly forward, thus
causing the palm to take a position that is neither posterior nor anterior, although partaking somewhat of the peculiarities of both [see cuts 17 and 18]. In the case of all
unrounded Vowel positions the terminal phalanges of the
thumb and accented finger overlap. In these it is possible
further to distinguish from one another the Back, Front,
and Mixed positions, by allowing the accented finger's

No. 17.
[VIEWED BY OBSERVER.]

No. 18.
[VIEWED BY OPERATOR.]

Low Mixed Primary Vowel.

terminal phalanx to come in contact with the back of the thumb, in the Back positions ; by allowing the accented finger's terminal phalanx to come in contact with the front of the thumb, in the Front positions ; and by allowing the accented finger's terminal phalanx to lie horizontally above and in contact with the upper side of the thumb, in Mixed positions [see cuts 16, 12, and 18, pages 26, 24, 26]. By thus placing the modifying phalanx of the finger back of the thumb's voice phalanx, when representing Back Vowels ; in front of it, when representing Front Vowels ; and in a compromising position, when representing Mixed Vowels ; the Manual is made to correspond very closely to the principles followed in the Visible Speech Vowel symbols.

General positions being provided to indicate the portion of the vocal organs employed to produce the Vowel sound, differentiations are resorted to, as in the treatment of Consonants, to represent the arrangement of the different parts at the points indicated by those general positions.

The terms High, Mid, and Low have reference to the elevation of the tongue at the point indicated by the general position of the hand. A High position of the tongue is indicated by accenting the third finger ; a Mid position of the tongue by accenting the middle finger ; and a Low position of the tongue by accenting the index finger. Here again a resemblance to the Visible Speech symbols crops out in the case of the Back Primary Vowels. It will be seen by an inspection of the Back Primary Vowel positions on the Chart that the terminal phalanges of the fingers, which are not directly back of the voice phalanx of the thumb, appear above it with High Vowels, below it with Low Vowels, and both above and below it with Mid Vowels [compare cuts 24, 20, and 22, pages 30, 28, 29].

All of the Vowel characteristics and the manner of their representation have now been explained. It, however, may be interesting to whoever has made a thorough study of Visible Speech, to see how the Back Primary Vowel positions are logically derived from the Vocalized Back Primary

Consonant position and its inner and outer varieties. It was deemed unnecessary to distinguish in the Manual between the inner, outer, and central or normal Consonant positions. In the representation of the Back Primary Consonant the inner variety is suggested by the position of the breath phalanx of the thumb [see cut 19]. When the breath phalanx of the thumb extends beyond the index-finger side of the hand we know that the breath is represented as passing into the nose ; so, when this phalanx lies barely within the palm, we know that the breath is modified by some part of the mouth, and, as this part of the mouth is logically as near as possible to the nasal passage, we see that the Consonant thus represented must correspond to the inner variety.

No. 19.
" Inner," Vocalized Back Primary
Consonant.

No. 20
Low Back Primary Vowel.

As there is nothing in this position to indicate that the Consonant is " Wide," or that it has any lip modification, it follows, that if it be allied to any Vowel, it must be to some Primary Vowel. We have seen that Consonant positions are distinguished generally from Vowel positions by the mode of accentuation ; so, in order to change this inner Back Primary Consonant position into a Primary Vowel position, we must replace the Consonant accentuation with a Vowel accentuation. To do this in the present instance. without shifting appreciably the position of the breath phalanx of the thumb. we must cause the accented voice phalanx of the thumb to overlap the terminal phalanx of the index finger. After this is done, and the unaccented fingers are allowed to close naturally, we shall find that the Low Back Primary Vowel is represented [see cut 20, page 28]. This is exactly as it should be. because the Vocalized inner Back Primary Consonant is allied to the Low Back Primary Vowel.

No. 21.
"Normal," Vocalized Back Primary Consonant.

No. 22.
Mid Back Primary Vowel, [u in up].

Again, take the same Consonant position, but bring the breath phalanx of the thumb farther into the palm, so that the voice phalanx will be directed toward the middle finger. and we shall have a correct representation of a central or normal Back Primary Consonant [see cut 21]. By transforming this into a Primary Vowel position, as was done in the case of the inner variety, a Mid Back Primary Vowel will be represented [see cut 22]. This is also as it should be, because the central or normal Vocalized Back Primary Consonant is allied to the Mid Back Primary Vowel.

Again, take the same Consonant position. but bring the breath phalanx still farther into the palm. so that the voice phalanx will be directed toward the third finger, and we shall have a correct representation of an outer Back Primary Consonant [see cut 23]. Proceeding as before, we shall find that there will be represented the Vowel which is allied to this variety of Consonants ; namely, the High Back Primary Vowel [see cut 24]. It will thus be seen that this allied relation of the several Back Primary Vowels to the Vocalized Back Primary Consonant and its inner and outer varieties, may be perfectly traced in accordance with a logical interpretation of the Manual, and the laws which govern its formation.

No. 23.
" Outer," Vocalized Back Primary
Consonant.

No. 24.
High Back Primary Vowel.

GLIDES.

Glides, as was stated, are intermediate to Consonants and Vowels, and possess in common with them marked characteristics. They are allied to certain central aperture Consonants, but are free from the compression or buzzing effect which is peculiar to Consonant sounds. On the other hand, they resemble Vowels in being produced with the channel expanded, but differ from them in not having a fixed configuration. It has been the aim, therefore, in the representation of the Glides or transitional sounds to make these various relations apparent. A reference to the Charts

will show that each Glide position differs from that of
its allied Consonant merely in the position of the breath
phalanx of the thumb, which in the former is held at an
angle to the plane of the palm, while in the latter it is held
parallel with the plane of the palm. Thus it will be seen
that the Glide position, though resembling in many respects
its allied Consonant position, does not, as viewed by the
operator, present the narrow or compressed feature common to Consonants, but rather suggests the expanded or
wide quality of Vowels [see cuts 25 and 26].

No. 25.
[VIEWED BY OBSERVER.]

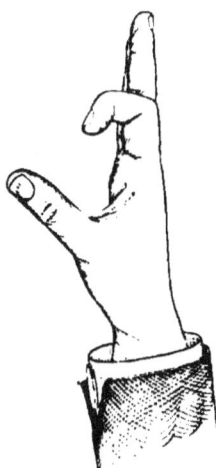

No. 26.
[VIEWED BY OPERATOR.]

Lip Mixed-Glide.

Sometimes a rounded Glide is allied to a Consonant
which shows no lip modification, as in the case with both
the Top and the Point Round-Glide. In order to represent
"Round" in these Glide positions the unaccented fingers
are permitted to assume a circular outline.

Glides, like Consonants, are classified into Throat, Back,
Top, Point, and Lip. So, the Throat, Back, and Top Glides
are considered posterior, and in representing them the palm
is held laterally at an angle to the fore-arm ; and the Point

32

and Lip Glides are considered anterior, and are represented with the palm held upright and in line with the arm. The several phalanges carry with them the same significance which attaches to them in the allied Consonant positions. Twelve Glides are represented, and this number might be readily increased in accordance with the rules given, if necessity for them should arise.

The following explanation of Glides and their relations to the other classes of speech sounds is adapted from Prof. Bell's

COMPLETE TABLE OF GLIDES.

NAME.	EXPLANATION.
Breath-Glide.	A transitional aspiration, of organic quality corresponding to that of the adjoining elements [= a soft effect of the Consonants, Back Primary ; Top Primary; Point Primary ; Lip Primary ; etc.]. Although this Glide has no fixed abiding place, and is of a somewhat variable organic formation, yet in its effect it is very closely allied to the Throat Consonant aspirate, and is therefore represented with a posterior position of the palm and a separation of the index and middle fingers, which are the characteristic features of Throat positions. This is the only non-vocal Glide, and hence is the only one in the representation of which the voice phalanx is unaccented.
Voice-Glide.	Vowel murmur [= a non-syllabic effect of the Mid Mixed Primary Vowel]. It is a Throat formation, and is shown to be so by the position which represents it.
Round-Glide.	Rounded murmur [= a non-syllabic effect of the Mid Mixed Primary Round Vowel]. This also is a Throat formation, and is represented by a position which suggests an unrepresented Vocalized Throat Mixed Consonant.

Throat-Glide.   A semi-vowelized sound of the Vocalized Throat Primary Consonant.

Back-Glide.   A semi-vowelized sound of the Vocalized Back Primary Consonant.

Back Mixed-Glide.   A semi-vowelized sound of the Vocalized Back Mixed Consonant.

Top-Glide.   A semi-vowelized sound of the Vocalized Top Primary Consonant.

Top Round-Glide.   A semi-vowelized sound of the Vocalized Top Primary Consonant with lip modification.

Point-Glide.   A semi-vowelized sound of the Vocalized Point Primary Consonant.

Point Round-Glide.   A semi-vowelized sound of the Vocalized Point Primary Consonant with lip modification.

Lip-Glide.   A semi-vowelized sound of the Vocalized Lip Primary Consonant.

Lip Mixed-Glide.   A semi-vowelized sound of the Vocalized Lip Mixed Consonant.

The Voice-Glide, Top-Glide, Point-Glide, and Lip Mixed-Glide are the only ones which are recognized as English linguistic elements.

Before leaving this class, attention should be called to a common difference which exists between the horizontal rows of Glides as they are arranged on the Chart. A very little reflection will show that the Glides represented in the upper row differ from corresponding Glides represented in the lower row, by having their production attended with a wider expansion of some part of the vocal organs. We may, therefore, very properly regard the relation, which the lower row of Glides bears to the upper row, as that of "Primary" to "Wide." The distinction to which attention has been directed, is not indicated on the Chart, nor is it anywhere set forth in Visible Speech. The sole utility of this classification of Glides into "Primary" and "Wide," will be found in our discussion of Glides-Indicated.

GLIDES-INDICATED.

We come now to the consideration of Glides-Indicated,
a class of positions which has no exact counterpart in Visible Speech, and which might be omitted from the Manual
without materially affecting its efficiency. These positions, which are twenty-four in number, have the phonetic
value of Glide positions, but are adapted to follow Vowel
positions with greater ease and smoothness. A series of
positions which may be glided into from Vowel positions,
so as to illustrate the easy transition from a Vowel to its
Glide, may very properly constitute a part of this Manual,
which is designed to represent to the eye the actual operation of the vocal organs. In the representation of Glides-
Indicated, the accented finger is always straightened, and
is accented by having the accented voice phalanx of the
thumb brought in contact with its second phalanx; thus
the composite qualities peculiar to Glide positions are contributed [see cuts 27 and 28]. This mode of accentuation
constitutes the distinguishing characteristic of the entire
class.

No. 27.
[VIEWED BY OBSERVER.]

No. 28.
[VIEWED BY OPERATOR.]

Primary Low Lip Glide-Indicated.

The positions shown on the Chart under Glides-Indicated
are subdivided into the Back, Top, Point, and Lip. These

subdivisions exhibit points of similarity to corresponding
subdivisions under Consonants and Glides. The Back and
Top positions are posterior, and the Point and Lip anterior,
as is shown by the position which the palm takes relatively
to the arm. It will be noted that the Top and Point positions have the voice phalanx of the thumb resting against
the side of the accented finger's second phalanx. This
brings the accented finger perpendicular to the palm, as was
found to be the case with the accented fingers in Top and
Point Consonants, and thus makes these positions especially
fitted to indicate Top and Point Glides [see cut 35, page 51].
It also will be noted that in the Back and Lip positions the
thumb presses the accented finger open so far as it is possible
to do so and still retain its place against the front of that
finger's second phalanx [see cuts 27 and 28, page 34]. This
forces the accented finger into a position which approxi-
mates, more or less closely, that of the accented fingers in
the case of Back and Lip Consonants, and thus makes
these positions especially fitted to indicate Back and Lip
Glides.

One half of the positions have the unaccented fingers
closed, and hence should be employed only to indicate
Glides which are "Primary," according to the classification
specified in the discussion of Glides. The other half of the
positions have straightened unaccented fingers, and therefore should be used only to replace those Glides which have
been classified as "Wide." The Primary or Wide feature of
the Glide-Indicated positions is not owing to the unelimi-
nated quality of the associated Vowel, which, for the sake of
convenience, has been allowed to enter into its composition,
but is made to depend wholly upon the "Primary" or
"Wide" nature of the Glide which is indicated. Hence, it
follows that each of these varieties may be properly used
with all varieties of Vowels.

Glides-Indicated resemble, in but a single particular, the
Vowels with which they are used. The associated Vowel
position always determines which finger shall receive the

accent. That is to say, when one of the Glides-Indicated is used with a High Vowel, as an initial or a finish, the third finger is accented ; when one of them is used with a Mid Vowel, the middle finger is accented ; and when one of them is used with a Low Vowel, the first or index finger is accented.

Although, from the very nature of the case, Glides-Indicated are non-descriptive of any specific action or adjustment of the vocal organs, yet they are in perfect accord with the rules and principles heretofore laid down, and each one accurately and unmistakably points out the Glide which it undertakes to indicate. A set of these positions has not been provided especially for the indication of the Glides which are formed in the throat ; but where, as in English, the Back Glides are never used, the Back Glides-Indicated may be safely and conveniently employed to indicate two such Glides. —one " Primary" and one "Wide."

To have these positions subserve the purpose for which they were devised, attention should be given to the way in which the transitions to or from them are made. Especially is this so when the palm also assumes a new position. When a posterior Glide-Indicated is used after a Front or a Mixed Vowel, which often happens, the palm should be carried into the posterior position at the same time that the accented finger is being straightened, and while the accented voice phalanx of the thumb is being brought, with a smooth gliding movement, into its proper place against the accented finger's second phalanx. A similar course should be pursued in assuming an anterior position after a Back or a Mixed Vowel.

The extent to which Glides shall in practice be replaced by Glides-Indicated is a matter which must be left to the discretion of the instructor. Experience, both in and out of the classroom, encourages the invariable use of this mode of representing the Top-Glide, and the Lip Mixed-Glide ; in English, the Point or R-Glide combines with the several Vowels in too varied a manner to be thus represented without danger of confusion.

A few words are called for in explanation of the symbols which appear in connection with this class of Manual positions. A set of new symbols became necessary ; because, as was stated at the beginning of this subdivision, nothing is found in Visible Speech which is the exact counterpart of Glides-Indicated. The intimate relation which they sustain to Glides has suggested the propriety of using, for this purpose, a modification of the Visible Speech Glide symbols. In all of the symbols of the Back. Top, Point, and Lip Glides a curve is a constant factor. By duplicating this curve in each instance, these Glide symbols are transformed into Glide-Indicated symbols. The location of the curves relatively to the perpendicular line determines whether the symbolized Glide-Indicated is High, Mid, or Low. Thus, a High Glide-Indicated is symbolized when both of these curves are placed at the top of the perpendicular line ; a Mid Glide-Indicated is symbolized when one curve is placed at the top and the other curve placed at the bottom of the perpendicular line ; and a Low Glide-Indicated is symbolized when both of the curves are placed at the bottom of the perpendicular line. One great advantage of this mode of symbolization is, that each time a Glide-Indicated is symbolized its cognate Glide is suggested.

NASALIZED TONES.

Thus far we have been considering the representation of speech sounds which were either oral or nasal. Oral sounds having a nasal quality, sometimes called Nasalized Tones, are often met with, however, both as linguistic elements and defects. It becomes necessary, therefore, to provide for their representation. If, while attempting the production of an oral sound, the soft palate is allowed to relax its pressure against the posterior wall of the pharynx, so as not to close the nasal passage, the voice will resound partly in the nose and partly in the mouth, and the oral sound will acquire a nasal quality. This nasal quality is indicated by gently twisting the hand in opposite directions so as to give it a slight but perceptible rotary motion, while it still retains the position which represents the fundamental oral adjustment. The rotary motion of the hand will necessarily be accompanied by a slight twisting motion of the fore-arm. [Compare Trill.] This expedient may seem rather arbitrary, yet it will be noticed that at the end of alternate oscillations the breath phalanx of the thumb approaches the position which it takes when indicating Nasality. It hardly requires to be stated that this semi-nasal effect might be shown in the case of all oral open-aperture Consonants by carrying the breath phalanx of the thumb out beyond the index-finger side of the palm.

ORINASALS.

When a Vowel is subjected to the nasalization above described, and that modification is accompanied with a guttural contraction, the original character of the Vowel is altered and there is produced what is known as an Orinasal. This constitutes a very common element in the French, Portuguese, and modern Indian languages. From the Vocalized Throat Primary Consonant which represents guttural contraction, we may derive a very appropriate Orinasal symbol by placing the breath phalanx of the thumb in the position for Nasality. This symbol acts retrospectively, so in representing an Orinasal we represent the Vowel in the usual way and immediately follow it with the Orinasal symbol.

TRILL.

The Trill is indicated by actuating the wrist joint so as to cause the hand rapidly to vibrate. This vibratory motion of the hand is exclusively owing to the action of the wrist joint, and is accomplished without any rotary motion of either the hand or the arm. [Compare Nasalized Tones.]

LINKED-POSITIONS.

Sounds are sometimes heard which require the simultaneous use of two of the Manual positions to describe the adjustment of the vocal organs in their production. To show that two positions are thus co-descriptive, or Linked, the hand is slightly elevated while assuming the first position, and then immediately and suddenly lowered, to take the second position. Linked-Positions should not be employed to represent what are known as Combinations. To represent these, the positions should follow each other in the ordinary way.

SYLLABIC ACCENTUATION.

In many languages, and especially in English, the meanings of words are made to depend very largely upon the selection of the syllable or syllables which shall receive the principal stress or accent. The Manual would be incomplete if this important principle was omitted. The accent may be indicated in the spelling of all words of more than one syllable ; or else, in accordance with Prof. Bell's rule, whenever it does not occur on the first syllable of the word. Syllabic Accentuation is indicated by retaining the position which represents the most prominent sound in the accented syllable, while the hand is being carried away from the operator with a slight but marked movement.

SUMMARY.

SPEECH sounds are divided into Consonants, Vowels. and Glides. Consonants have a narrow or obstructed channel ; Vowels have an expanded and tense channel ; Glides partake somewhat of the nature of both Consonants and Vowels. The organic differences between Consonants, Vowels, and Glides are hinted at, when the several classes of positions are viewed from the index-finger side of the hand, and the accented fingers considered. The positions are to a certain extent mono-symbolic.

The palm held at an angle to the arm indicates a posterior position, and the palm held upright and in line with the arm an anterior position.

The thumb's second and terminal phalanges have a general and constant signification. When the second or breath phalanx extends beyond and out of contact with the index-finger side of the hand, the breath is shown to pass into the nose ; in any other position, it indicates that the breath passes into the mouth. When the breath is accompanied with voice, the terminal or voice phalanx of the thumb is accented ; otherwise, it is unaccented.

Straightened unaccented fingers simply signify "Wide."

CONSONANTS.

Consonant positions are distinguished by having the breath phalanx of the thumb close to the plane of the palm and the accented fingers straightened. When the voice phalanx of the thumb is accented, it is never held in contact with an accented finger's second, or with its terminal, phalanx. The Shut and Nasal positions under this class are the only positions which fail to have accented fingers.

In reading a Consonant position we begin at the index-finger side of the hand and treat as accented the nearest straightened finger, and also all other straightened fingers which are directly or indirectly in contact therewith ; and as unaccented, all fingers which are closed, and also all straightened fingers which are out of contact with an accented finger.

Non-Vocal Consonant positions have the voice phalanx of the thumb bent at right angles to the breath phalanx, or unaccented.

Vocalized Consonant positions have the voice phalanx of the thumb accented ; that is, brought in line with the breath phalanx : this constitutes the only difference between the Vocalized and analogous Non-Vocal Consonant positions.

Throat, Back, and Top Consonant positions, being posterior, have the palm held laterally at an angle to the arm.

Point and Lip Consonant positions, being anterior, have the palm upright and in line with the arm.

Back and Lip Consonant positions have the lower phalanges of the fingers in the plane of the palm.

Top and Point Consonant positions have the lower phalanges of the fingers at right angles to the plane of the palm.

Throat Consonant positions differ from those of the Back in having the index and middle fingers separated.

The first and second fingers, when accented, describe the aperture. The third and fourth fingers, when accented, mean Mixed. The thumb s second phalanx, when carried beyond and out of contact with the index-finger side of the hand, denotes Nasality. Hence :—

Primary Consonant positions have only the first finger accented.

Mixed Consonant positions have the second, third, and fourth fingers accented.

Divided Consonant positions have the first and second fingers accented.

Mixed-Divided Consonant positions have all of the fingers accented.

Shut Consonant positions do not have any of the fingers accented.

Nasal Consonant positions have the breath phalanx of the thumb in the position to indicate Nasality. None of the fingers are accented.

There are fifty-two Consonant positions.

VOWELS.

Vowel positions are distinguished by always having the voice phalanx of the thumb accented and in contact with the terminal phalanx of the accented finger. This kind of accent is the strongest which can be given a finger, and so always takes precedence. Two modes of accentuation may not co-exist.

In Primary Vowel positions the accented voice phalanx of the thumb and the terminal phalanx of the accented finger overlap. None of the unaccented fingers are straightened.

Wide Vowel positions differ from analogous Primary Vowel positions by having straightened unaccented fingers, to denote " Wide."

Round Vowels differ visibly from normal aperture Vowels by having a contraction of the labial aperture. This is shown by bringing the terminal phalanges of the thumb and the accented finger together so as to form an outline which is approximately round.

Back Vowels have the palm in the posterior position.

Front Vowels have the palm in the anterior position.

Mixed Vowels have the palm thrown forward so as to assume a compromising position.

When the voice phalanx and the terminal phalanx of the accented finger overlap, the Back. Front. and Mixed Vowel positions are further distinguished by having the terminal phalanx of that finger in contact with the back of the thumb's voice phalanx, in Back positions ; in front of it, in Front positions ; and above it, in Mixed positions.

The terms High, Mid, and Low refer to the elevation of the tongue at the place indicated by the general position of the hand.

High Vowels have the third finger accented.

Mid Vowels have the middle finger accented.

Low Vowels have the first or index finger accented.

By a logical interpretation of the Manual and the laws which govern its formation, the allied relation of the several Back Primary Vowels to the Vocalized Back Primary Consonant and its inner and outer varieties, may be perfectly traced.

The Vowel positions are thirty-six in number.

GLIDES.

Glide positions are distinguished by having the breath phalanx of the thumb held at an angle to the plane of the palm. The voice phalanx of the thumb is never in contact with a finger.

Glides are intermediate to Consonants and Vowels, and the organic relation to them is illustrated by the Glide positions when a lateral view of them is taken.

The hand is read in the same manner as in the case of Consonant positions, and the same value is given to both accented and unaccented fingers.

When rounded Glides are allied to Consonants having no lip modification, " Round " is shown by permitting the unaccented fingers to assume a circular outline.

Twelve Glide positions are given, and this number might be easily increased if necessity should arise. There are but four English Glides.

As arranged on the Chart, the relation of the Glides in the lower row to corresponding ones in the upper row may be considered, in a certain sense, that of " Primary " to " Wide." This distinction has its sole utility in connection with Glides-Indicated.

GLIDES-INDICATED.

Glide-Indicated positions are distinguished by having the accented finger straightened, and the accented voice phalanx of the thumb in contact with that finger's second phalanx. They are adapted to illustrate the easy transition from Vowel to Glide. Glides-Indicated possess exactly the same phonetic value and significance as the Glides which they respectively replace.

These positions are subdivided into Back, Top, Point, and Lip. Of these, the Back and Lip positions exhibit points of similarity to Back and Lip Consonant positions, and are thus fitted to indicate Back and Lip Glides. On the other hand, the Top and Point Glides-Indicated are shown, by a parity of reasoning, to be especially fitted to indicate Top and Point Glides.

One half of the positions have closed unaccented fingers, and hence should be employed only to indicate " Primary " Glides ; while the other half have straightened unaccented fingers, and hence should be employed only to indicate " Wide " Glides. The " Primary " or " Wide " quality of Glides-Indicated is not derived from the associated Vowel, but is purely descriptive of the Glide which is indicated. Consequently, so far as this quality is concerned, Glides-Indicated may be used indiscriminately with all varieties of Vowels.

Glides-Indicated, when used with a High Vowel, have the third finger accented ; when used with a Mid, the middle finger ; and when used with a Low, the first finger. In no other particular are they influenced by the associated Vowel. Although they are non-descriptive of any specific action or arrangement of the vocal organs, they afford a way of indicating the ease and smoothness of the mechanical transition from one vocal adjustment to another, and at the same time unmistakably point out the Glides which they undertake to indicate ; these Glides explicitly describe, in their turn, the organic formation of the sounds.

When, as in English, the Back-Glides are never employed, the Back Glides-Indicated may be safely used to indicate two of the Glides which are formed in the throat. Care should be exercised in assuming these positions to make them subserve the purpose for which they were devised.

Experience encourages the invariable use of Glides-Indicated for the Top-Glide and the Lip Mixed-Glide, but not for the Point or R-Glide.

The symbols which are used with this class of positions differ from the Visible Speech Glide symbols in having the curve duplicated. The location of the curves relatively to the perpendicular line determines whether the Glide-Indicated is High, Mid, or Low.

There are twenty-four Glide-Indicated positions.

It is not necessary to summarize Nasalized Tones, Orinasals, Trill, Linked-Positions, and Syllabic Accentuation. Ample consideration has already been accorded them on pages 37, 38, and 39.

One hundred and twenty-five positions are embraced in the Manual.

POSITIONS ANALYZED.

W̲E will now examine a few Manual positions in the light of the preceding discussion, and try to interpret them. In each instance we will first determine whether the given position is a Consonant, Vowel, Glide, or Glide-Indicated, and then by reading it in accordance with the rules that obtain in the class to which it belongs, discover its place and meaning.

Let us consider the position shown in cut 29. We see it cannot belong to Vowels or Glides-Indicated because the voice phalanx of the thumb is unaccented. Neither is it a Glide position because the breath phalanx of the thumb is not held at an angle to the plane of the palm. The position, if it be a Manual position, must therefore come under the head of Consonants. As the unaccented voice phalanx of the thumb can never be employed to accent a finger, the straightened fingers here must be accented fingers ; and we perceive that the position answers to the general requirements of Consonant positions, which are, that the thumb's breath phalanx shall lie close to the plane of the palm, and that all of the accented fingers shall be straightened. Having determined the class to which this position belongs, we are now ready to consider its meaning. It is Non-Vocal because the voice phalanx of the thumb is unaccented. It represents some posterior position because the palm is held at an angle to the arm : the one represented,.

must be a Top position because that class of posterior positions alone is represented with the first or lower phalanges
of the fingers at right angles to the palm. It is a central
aperture Consonant because, the index finger not being
straightened, there can be only one of the aperture fingers
accented. It is Mixed because the third and fourth fingers
are accented. Hence, the position shown in cut 29 represents the Non-Vocal Top Mixed Consonant.

No 29.
Non-Vocal Top Mixed
Consonant,
[sb in wish].

No. 30.
Vocalized Point Divided
Consonant,
[l in rail].

The position shown in cut 30 cannot belong to Vowels
because the voice phalanx of the thumb, though accented,
is not in contact with a finger's terminal phalanx. It cannot belong to Glides because the breath phalanx of the
thumb fails to stand at an angle to the plane of the palm.
It cannot belong to Glides-Indicated because the voice
phalanx of the thumb, though accented, is not held in contact with a finger's second phalanx. This position must
be, therefore, a Consonant position if it belong to the Manual. Moreover, the breath phalanx of the thumb is close to
the plane of the palm ; the thumb's accented voice phalanx
is not in contact with a finger's second, or with its terminal, phalanx ; and the accented fingers are straightened :
hence, we see that this position corresponds perfectly to
the requirements of Consonant positions. It is Vocalized

because the terminal phalanx of the thumb is accented, showing that the breath is accompanied with voice. It represents some anterior position because the palm is upright and in line with the arm : the one represented, must be a Point position because that class of anterior positions alone is represented with the first or lower phalanges of the fingers at right angles to the palm. It is Divided because both the first and the second fingers are accented, which shows that the aperture consists of a double opening. Putting all these facts together, we find that the position shown in cut 30 represents the Vocalized Point Divided Consonant.

In the position shown in cut 31, the voice phalanx of the thumb is accented and overlaps the terminal phalanx of the index finger. Consequently this position cannot belong to Consonants, Glides, or Glides-Indicated. If it were a Consonant position the voice phalanx of the thumb, being accented, would not be in contact with a finger's second, or with its terminal, phalanx. If it were a Glide position the voice phalanx of the thumb would not be brought in contact with any finger. If it were one of the Glide-Indicated positions the accented finger would be straightened, and the accented voice phalanx of the thumb would be in contact with that finger's second phalanx. As this position then corresponds only to the requirements of Vowel positions, which are that the voice phalanx of the thumb shall be accented and shall be in contact with the terminal phalanx of the accented finger, we know that the position under consideration is a Vowel position. It represents a Primary Vowel because the accented voice phalanx of the thumb and the terminal phalanx of the accented finger overlap, and there is an absence of straightened unaccented fingers. It is a Front position because the palm is upright and in line with the arm to denote an anterior position, and also because the terminal phalanx of the accented finger comes in contact with the front of the thumb's voice phalanx. It is a Low position because the first or index finger is the one which is accented. Hence, the position shown in cut 31 represents the Low Front Primary Vowel.

No. 31.
Low Front Primary Vowel,
[e in net].

No. 32.
High Back Wide Round Vowel,
[oo in foot].

For the same reasons as were stated in connection with the preceding position, the position shown in cut 32 also must represent a Vowel. It is a Back Vowel because the palm is held at an angle to the arm, which denotes a posterior position. It describes a Round Vowel because the tips of the terminal phalanges of the thumb and accented finger, in coming in contact, form an outline which is approximately round. It represents a Wide Vowel because there are straightened unaccented fingers. It is a High Vowel because the third finger is the accented finger. Hence, the position shown in cut 32 represents the High Back Wide Round Vowel.

In the position shown in cut 33, the thumb's breath phalanx is at an angle to the plane of the palm, and neither it nor the voice phalanx is held in contact with any finger. It is doubly evident, therefore, that this must be a Glide position. It is an anterior position because the palm is held upright and in line with the arm. It must be a Lip position because that class of anterior positions alone is represented with the first or lower phalanges of the fingers in the same plane as the palm. That the aperture is single and central is shown by the fact that only one of the aperture fingers is accented, the first being bent and therefore unaccented. It is Mixed because the third and fourth fingers are accented. Hence, the position shown in cut 33 represents the Lip Mixed-Glide.

No. 33.
Lip Mixed-Glide.

No. 34.
Point-Glide, [r in far].

Cut 34 represents a Glide position for the reasons given at the beginning of the foregoing paragraph. It is also clearly evident that it is a Point position and that it is Primary. Hence, cut 34 represents the Point or R-Glide.

The position shown in cut 35 will readily be identified as one of the Glide-Indicated positions from the fact, that the accented finger is straightened, and that the voice phalanx of the thumb, which is accented, is brought in contact with this finger's second phalanx. The position is shown to be posterior by the angle which the palm takes relatively to the arm. A Top position is here indicated because the accented finger is held at right angles to the palm, as is the case with the accented finger in Top Consonant and Top-Glide positions. It is Wide because it has a straightened unaccented finger. That it should be used with some Mid Vowel is made apparent by having the middle finger

accented.   Hence, the position shown in cut 35 represents the
Wide Mid Top Glide-Indicated.   In other words, this position should be used only with Mid Vowel positions to indicate the Top-Glide, which is commonly called the Y-Glide.
This position may be properly used to represent the second
element of *a* in dame, and the second element of *i* in d*i*me.

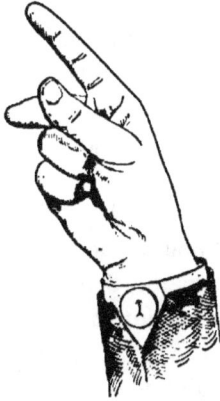

No. 35.
Wide Mid Top Glide-Indicated.

PRINCIPAL AIMS.

ATTENTION is constantly being called to the unphonetic character of orthographic English, and to the difficulties which necessarily arise from the fact in teaching the deaf to speak. Our spelling is not only unphonetic, but its inconsistencies occasion endless confusion in the mind of the child. Much time and thought have been devoted to the revising of old methods and the devising of new ones, whereby a knowledge of spoken language could be imparted. A prerequisite to the use of spoken words is a knowledge of the order and phonetic value of the elements which enter into them, just as an appreciation of the meaning and value of musical notation is a prerequisite to singing by note. Although such a knowledge will not of itself make speakers of the deaf, yet it is fundamental in its nature. Long, constant, and patient exercise of the vocal organs alone can give dexterity and a degree of naturalness : but the ability to produce intelligibly the elementary linguistic sounds will not avail, unless the pupil has also a clear conception of the phonetic elements as combined in the particular word which he wishes to utter. I believe that to the vague, uncertain, and incorrect notion in the mind of the deaf may be attributed a very large share of their vague, uncertain, and incorrect pronunciation and articulation. Experience has shown that we are too often inclined to make the vocal organs responsible for errors which are owing wholly to a misconception in the mind of the child regarding the phonetic principles which should be employed, or their arrangement. In such cases the vocal organs may be perfectly obedient, and may be correctly reflecting the pupil's false or imperfect notion of the combination which he desires to use, so that a correction of the false and imperfect notion will be followed by a correction of his mispronunciation and faulty articulation. One of the principal objects of this Manual is to provide a practical method of giving to the deaf a full and correct apprehension of words as they are spoken. Another object aimed at, is the providing of convenient means whereby a satisfactory idea of the mechanical formation of speech sounds may be conveyed. From the very nature of speech and its production, a great deal of the mechanical formation of speech sounds is partly or wholly concealed. A convenient mode, therefore, of suggestively symbolizing these hidden actions will be found of great utility in giving to the deaf that clear and adequate conception of the manner of producing speech sounds, which must necessarily be the ·foundation of all intelligible and acceptable articulation. This Manual has, then, these two aims principally in view:—first, the imparting of a practical and abiding knowledge of the exact combinations of phonetic elements used in spoken words ; and secondly, the furnishing of a clear and accurate representation of the manner in which those elementary sounds are physiologically produced.

The Manual is undoubtedly qualified to achieve these aims, provided there are no intrinsic reasons tending to show that it is impracticable. But two such reasons, I apprehend, may be possibly urged :—that it is too scientific and technical ; and also that the positions are too difficult for the hand easily to assume. The description of the Manual is necessarily scientific and technical because the analysis which it follows and illustrates is pre-eminently scientific. The description herein given, however, is not intended for the pupil, but for the instructor. It is very desirable that the instructor should thoroughly understand the whole system, but the deaf child may use the Manual with profit without fully understanding a single principle upon which it rests. He articulates many sounds without perfectly understanding the functions of the vocal organs, so he may be permitted to represent those sounds by the proper Manual positions before he understands the full meaning of the positions, or even that they symbolize the vocal adjustment. Sooner or later he will learn that the Manual positions are descriptive, and then he will discover that he possesses the reliable key to a spoken language,— a key which he can never forget, nor mislay. He will find that he has been unconsciously acquiring a practical knowledge of phonetic combinations, and also of the functions of the vocal organs in producing the words which he would gladly speak ; and thus has overcome, without effort, the two great obstacles to the use of spoken words. Furthermore, Visible Speech has been found of great assistance in the oral training of the deaf, and an objection which cannot avail against Visible Speech can hardly hold good as against the Manual which exemplifies it. As to the Manual positions being difficult to take, it only need be said that no pupil has been found who could not, after a little practice, readily and satisfactorily assume any of them. That there are really no valid intrinsic reasons why the Manual may not be successfully employed to attain the aims above stated, is conclusively shown by the fact that all the pupils, without a single exception, who received instruction in the Manual, soon became able to carry on conversation by means of it, and voluntarily began to use it in place of the common manual alphabet.

PRACTICAL WORKINGS.

THE practical application of some of the principles which
have been elaborated, may help to a clearer understanding of the Manual and will afford an opportunity to consider
a few facts which have not elsewhere claimed our attention.

A necessary preliminary to any practical use of the Manual is the selection of a code of elementary sounds. In con-
structing such a code each one may exercise, to a certain
degree, his own judgement, and may decide for himself in
regard to the number and character of the sounds which may
be satisfactorily employed in the formation of the words he
purposes to represent. The Code of English Sounds which
is here submitted for the purpose of illustrating the Manual,
has been subjected to a thorough experimental test, both in
and out of the classroom, and has been found to be convenient
and adequate. The aim has been to make it conform neither to an extremely nice, nor to an extremely free, analysis ; but to have it, so far as possible, devoted exclusively to
the sounds which correct speakers use in their unstudied
utterance of words in ordinary conversation. By doing this
the number of Manual positions required, are neither so
numerous as to confuse and discourage the pupil, nor so
meagre as to make him careless and inexact.

A careful examination of the exercises on page 57, will
speedily give a practical knowledge of the Manual, even to
those who are not conversant with Visible Speech and have
found it difficult to understand the theory of the system.

CODE OF ENGLISH SOUNDS.

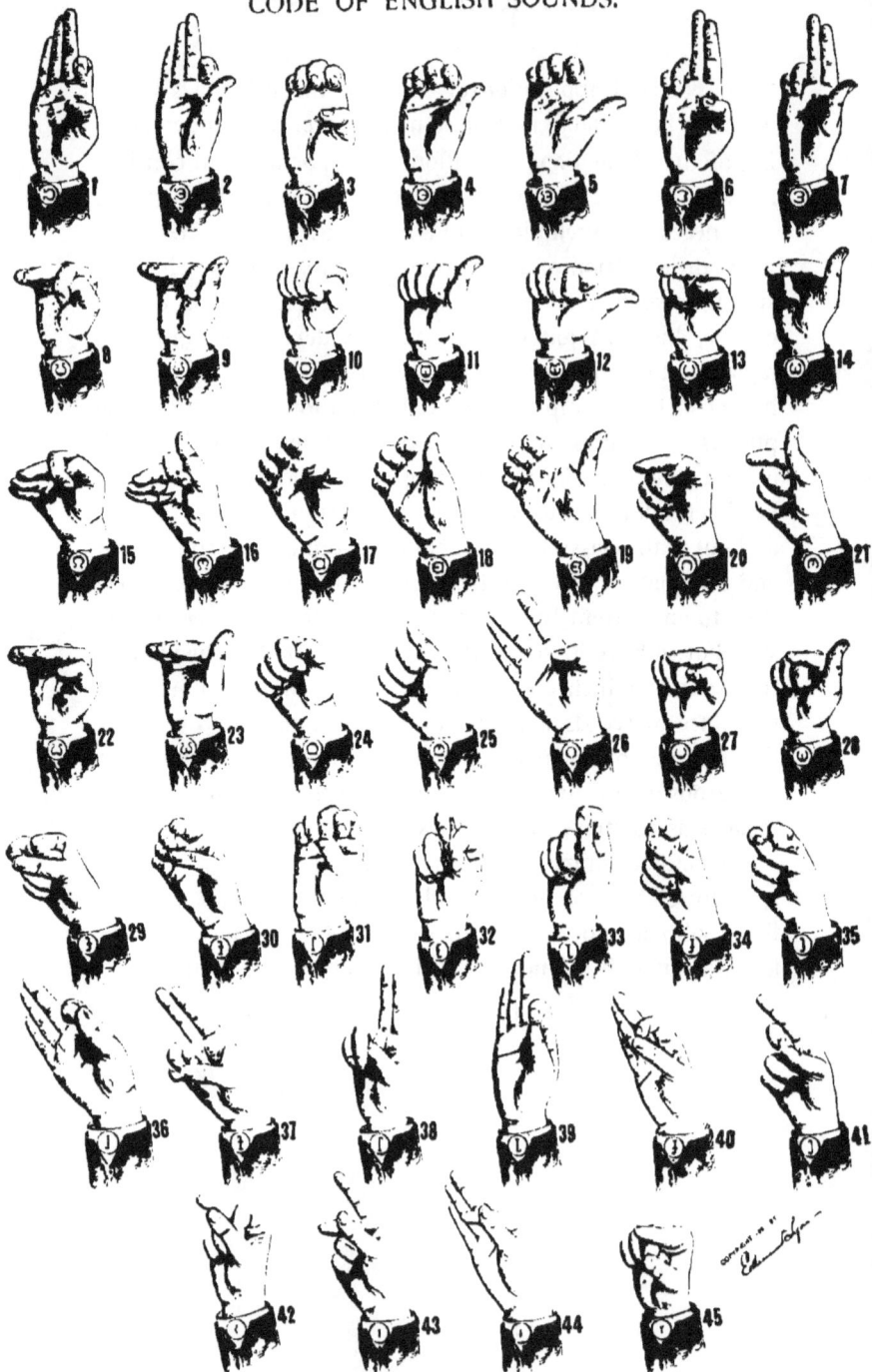

*KEY-WORDS ILLUSTRATING THE CODE.

17 39 3	17 39 4	17 39 5	22 34 10	22 27 30	23 30 10
ca p†	c a b	c a m	th ou *gh* t	th r ou *gh*	th a t

17 39 10	17 39 11	17 30 12	33 12 35 6	8 36 5	21 40 10
c a t	c a d	c a n	e n ou gh	*p* s a *l* m	y a *ch* t

4 39 17	4 39 18	4 39 19	28 35 6	3 13 41-42	11 29-42
b a ck	b a g	b a ng'	r ou gh	p l ou *gh*	d ou *gh*

30 12 34-44	12 32-43	12 41-43	12 41-42	12 29-42	12 21-30
a nn oy	n ay	n i *gh*	n ow	n o	n ew

14 31 10-15‡	14 31 11-16‡	17 1 35 8 10	10 1 38 10	11 2 34 45 6	8 31 9
l ee ch	l ie *g e*	q u e s t	t w i t	d w a r f	s ee s

14 39 17 8	14 39 18 9	1 33 10	2 33 10	28 30 15	28 30 16
l a x	l a g s	wh e t	w e t	r u ch *e*	r ou g *e*

2 38 15	2 38 22	2 38 23	14 31 6	14 31 7	31 9 38
w i sh	w i th *e*	w i th	l ea f	l ea v *e*	ea s y

3 13 40 10	4 14 40 10	21 29 45	29 29 45	10 27 32-43	11 28 32-43
p l o t	b l o t	y o r *e*	r oa r	t r ay	d r ay

26 35 10	36 45 5	6 30 11	6 37 10	8 31 10	8 38 10
h u t	a r m	f oo d	f oo t	s ea t	s i t

14 33 11 8	14 39 11	12 34 10	12 40 10	11 35 12 8 1	11 41 12 8
l e d	l a d	n au *gh* t	n o t	d u n c *e*	d a n c *e*

21 33 8	22 30 19 17	21-30	41-43	39 5	2 33 14
y e s	th a n k	you	I	a m	w e ll

3 13 31 9	18 38 7	5 31	22 38 19 17	23 33 12	30 17 10
p l ea s *e*	g i v *e*	m e	th i n k	th e n	a c t

---

* Pages 58 and 59 should be read before spelling out these exercises.

† Spell these nine underscored words, first as horizontally arranged, and then as perpendicularly arranged, and compare carefully the terminal positions.

‡ Good results are often obtained by employing 24-15 to represent the sound of *ch* in *leech*, and by employing 25-16 to represent the sound of *g* in *liege* and the sound of *j* in *join*.

§ Position 33 may be employed also to represent the Vowel sounds in *there*, *where*, and *air*.

‖ Position 35 may be satisfactorily used when the Vowel sound is indefinite, and when a strict analysis might require the use of the Voice-Glide or the Low Mixed Wide Vowel.

Key-words are at best unsatisfactory, and the deaf student who has occasion to study those given here should be especially careful not to associate the Manual positions with any of the letters used in orthographic spelling, but should strive to associate them in every instance with the vocal adjustment which they describe. To think that position 2=*w* would be utterly incorrect and would induce great confusion when such words as *now*, *know*, *quest*, and *twit*, were to be phonetically spelled. Those who most fully appreciate the fact that the Manual positions always describe the formation of the speech sounds, and never represent letters, will enjoy most fully the benefits of the system.

The figures which are placed above the words on the preceding page refer to the Manual positions shown in the Code of English Sounds. The letters which are printed in *italics* are silent ; that is, have no phonetic value. All of the groups of letters which are not italicized are treated as single elements, and for each of these groups there is a corresponding reference number. When the element consists of a diphthong, or of Consonants in combination, two numbers have to be employed to designate the required Manual positions. All such numbers are united by hyphens.

The positions from 1 to 28 inclusive are Consonant representations, and those from 29 to 41 inclusive represent Vowel formations. The position 42 is the Primary Mid Lip Mixed Glide-Indicated, the position 43 is the Wide Mid Top Glide-Indicated, the position 44 is the Wide Low Top Glide-Indicated, and the position 45 is the Point-Glide. The use of these Glide-Indicated positions does not necessarily involve any change in the way of writing Visible Speech by those who have become accostomed to the Glide symbolization of Prof. A. Melville Bell or of Dr. A. Graham Bell. When their Glide symbols are retained it may be well to place an accent, or some other mark, near the middle of the symbols which are used to represent positions 42 and 43, and at or near the bottom of the symbol which is used to represent position 44.

All of the Code positions appear also in their proper places among the Manual positions represented in the Charts which begin with page 62. They may be studied there to good advantage as they can be easily compared with allied and unallied positions, and a clear idea obtained regarding the correct arrangement of the different parts of the hand, and regarding the significance of the parts when so arranged.

In taking these Manual positions care should be exercised to indicate unmistakably the essential difference between the non-vocal and the vocalized speech sounds. The rule which is stated at the top of page 23 has this mainly in view, and should be strictly observed unless some accident or other cause has deprived the operator of full control over the thumb's terminal phalanx, so that it is impossible for him to assume properly the non-vocal position. In such cases the rule may be relaxed and the position of the thumb shown in cut 21 on page 29 may be employed to indicate a non-vocal speech sound.

A few facts worthy of passing notice are suggested by the sequence of the Manual positions as shown in the analysis of the words on page 57. In the initial combinations which occur in the words *tray* (10 27 32-43), *dray* (11 28 32-43), *clad* (17 13 39 11), *glad* (18 14 39 11), etc., the second Consonant is non-vocal when the first Consonant is non-vocal, and is vocalized when the first Consonant is vocalized. This rule may be easily impressed upon the pupil's mind by giving him to understand that in these and in similar cases, where the second Consonant is not disjoined from the first Consonant, the position which the thumb's terminal phalanx takes in representing the first Consonant must be retained while representing the second Consonant. Another fact which is illustrated by a practical use of the Manual is, that whenever the vocal transitions are smooth and easy the Manual transitions are smooth and easy ; *e. g.:* *mists* (53 8 10 8), *strands* (8 10 27 39 12 11 9) ; and that whenever the vocal transitions are less easy the Manual transitions correspond ; *e. g.:* *aches* (32-43 17 8), *exit* (33 17 8 38 10), *eggs* (33 18 9), *exact* (33 18 9 39 17 10).

It is possible that some statement may be expected, under the head of Practical Workings, regarding the value of the Manual and the benefits which have attended its adoption. A recital of the gratifying results which have crowned the use of the Manual thus far, and an account of the efficient way in which it has aided lip reading and has encouraged better articulation might be interesting and persuasive, but they may not be indulged in at this time. The pleasant and especial duty assigned me was to impart a practical understanding of the Manual and its governing principles, and with my earnest though imperfect attempt to do this my task must end.

CHARTS

OF

THE UNIVERSAL MANUAL.

NON-VOCAL CONSONANTS.

62

NASAL.

SHUT.

MIXED-DIVIDED.

DIVIDED.

MIXED.

POINT.

LIP.

PRIMARY.

VOCALIZED CONSONANTS.

NASAL.

SHUT.

MIXED-DIVIDED.

DIVIDED.

MIXED.

PRIMARY.

BACK.

TOP.

NASAL.

SHUT.

MIXED-DIVIDED.

DIVIDED.

MIXED.

POINT.   LIP.   PRIMARY.

THROAT CONSONANTS.

VOCALIZED PRIMARY.

NON-VOCAL SHUT.

NON-VOCAL PRIMARY.

ORINASAL SYMBOL.

NON-VOCAL PRIMARY.

GLIDES.

LIP-GLIDE.

POINT-GLIDE.

TOP-GLIDE.

BACK-GLIDE.

VOICE-GLIDE.

BREATH-GLIDE.

LIP MIXED-GLIDE.

POINT MIXED-GLIDE.

TOP MIXED-GLIDE.

BACK MIXED-GLIDE.

THROAT-GLIDE.

ROUND-GLIDE.

68

VOWELS.
(NORMAL APERTURE.)

BACK PRIMARY.　　BACK WIDE.　　MIXED PRIMARY.　　MIXED WIDE.　　FRONT PRIMARY.　　FRONT WIDE

HIGH.

FRONT WIDE.

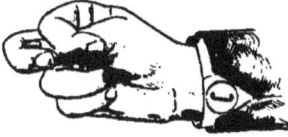

FRONT PRIMARY.

MIXED WIDE.

MIXED PRIMARY.

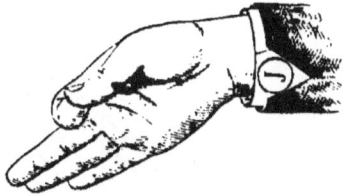

BACK WIDE.

MID.

LOW.

BACK PRIMARY.

ROUND VOWELS.

FRONT WIDE.

FRONT PRIMARY

MIXED WIDE.

MIXED PRIMARY.

BACK WIDE.

BACK PRIMARY.

HIGH.

FRONT WIDE.

FRONT PRIMARY.

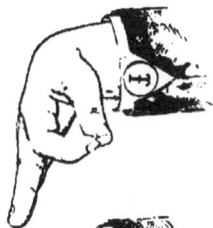

MIXED WIDE.

MIXED PRIMARY.

BACK WIDE.

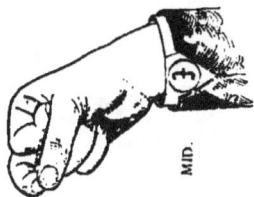

MID.

LOW.

BACK PRIMARY.

GLIDES-INDICATED.

| HIGH PRIMARY. | HIGH WIDE. | MID PRIMARY. | MID WIDE. | LOW PRIMARY. | LOW WIDE. |

     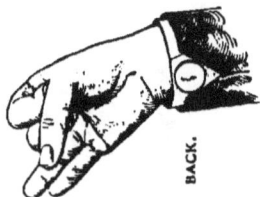

BACK.

TOP.

73

LOW WIDE

LOW PRIMARY.

MID WIDE.

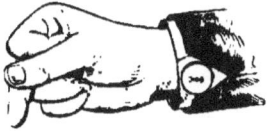

MID PRIMARY.

HIGH WIDE.

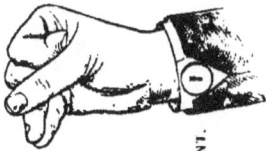

POINT.

UP.

HIGH PRIMARY